CAVES

Written by
Kerry Harwood

Caves are underground spaces that form when soft rock, such as limestone or sandstone, is eroded over thousands of years. They can also form from volcanic activity or when ice melts. They can be found all over the planet. Some caves are very big. Some of the longest caves are over 400 miles in length!

Caves can be home to interesting animals, such as bats, blind fish and cave crickets. Caves can also contain beautiful rock shapes, such as stalactites and stalagmites. Some caves can be explored on foot, while some need equipment to access them, like rappelling gear or scuba diving kit.

Caves can be tricky to navigate. If you get lost inside a cave, you might never be able to escape! It's important to explore them with an expert who is trained in cave safety and knows the layout of the cave.

Stalactites and stalagmites

Stalactites and stalagmites are spectacular rock outcrops that can be found inside caves.

Stalactites and stalagmites form when drops of rain find their way into a cave, collecting minerals on their way.

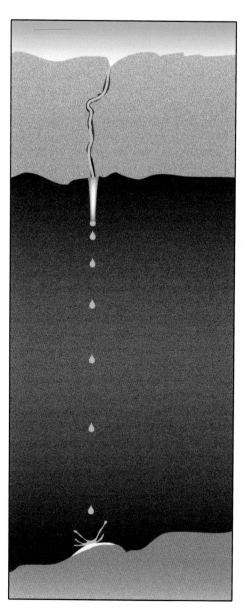

These droplets then evaporate, leaving behind deposits of minerals that gradually grow over time. It can take a very long time for them to form.

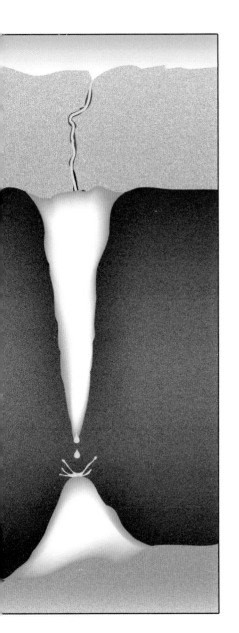
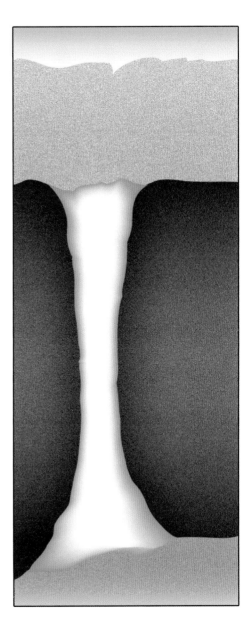

Stalactites hang from the roof of the cave and can look like icicles or long, thin cones. They can reach impressive sizes, up to 30m long. Stalactites grow very slowly, sometimes only a few cm every 100 years. Some are more than 190,000 years old!

Stalagmites, on the other hand, grow up from the cave floor and look like pillars, cones or even mushrooms. They form when droplets fall from the cave roof to the floor, then leave behind mineral deposits. Like stalactites, stalagmites grow very slowly and are able to reach remarkable sizes.

As stalactites grow down and stalagmites grow up, they can sometimes meet in the middle to form a tower. They take thousands of years to form and are often very beautiful.

Caves are home to a variety
of animals that have adapted
to their dark and damp
surroundings. Some of these
animals include:

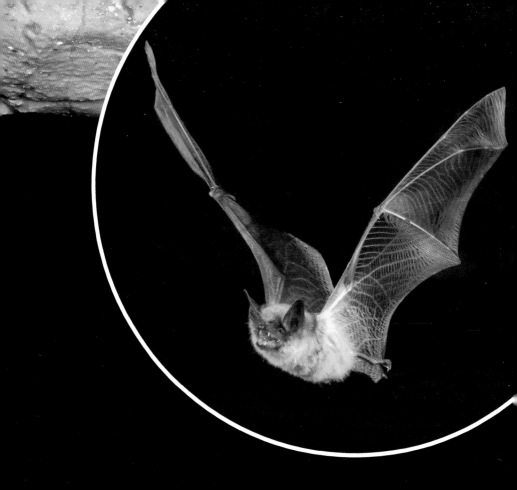

Bats

Bats are perhaps the most well-known animals that live in caves. They use sonar to navigate in the dark and can be found roosting in caves in the daytime. Bats feed on the insects that live in caves.

Blind Fish

Some fish that live in caves have evolved to be completely blind, as they don't need eyes to navigate in the dark. Instead, they feel their way around the cave and use their sense of smell to find food and mates.

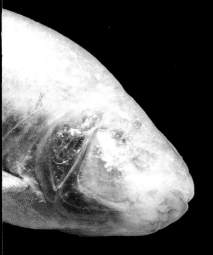

Cave Crickets

These insects are found in caves around the globe and have evolved to be perfectly adapted to their underground habitat. They have extra long legs that help them to jump long distances.

Olm

The olm is an aquatic salamander. It has adapted to living in the dark and moist surroundings of caves. Olms have long, slender bodies and lack eyes or pigment, as they don't need to see or be hidden in the dark.

Spiders

Some spiders have adapted to living in caves, where they can find plenty of food and shelter. These spiders have developed elongated legs and sensitive hairs to help them feel their way around in the dark.

Cave millipedes

These arthropods are found in caves all over the planet and have adapted to their dark, damp habitat. They have long, segmented bodies and can roll up to protect themselves from predators.

The animals that live in caves are incredibly diverse and have adapted to survive in their dark and often harsh surroundings.

Most cave-dwelling animals are harmless to humans, but it's important to remember that they may be sensitive to disturbance and easily harmed. Therefore, we must explore caves responsibly and with care.

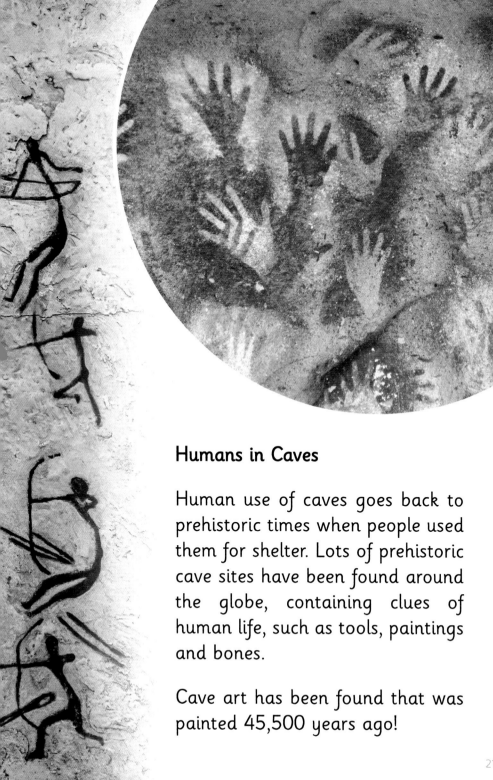

Humans in Caves

Human use of caves goes back to prehistoric times when people used them for shelter. Lots of prehistoric cave sites have been found around the globe, containing clues of human life, such as tools, paintings and bones.

Cave art has been found that was painted 45,500 years ago!

Spelunking

Exploring caves for fun or sport is called 'spelunking'. The word comes from the Latin word *spelunca*, which means 'cave'. It can be a very exciting and intrepid activity.

Some spelunkers enjoy taking photographs or creating maps of the caves they explore.

Spelunking has different levels of difficulty, from easy treks in large dry caves to extreme climbs into icy passages and bottomless pits.

When you go spelunking, you need to wear gear like helmets, headlamps and knee pads to keep you safe while crawling between tight gaps and climbing over rocks. You'll need to remember some extra clothes and snacks, because spelunking can take a long time and you must not get hungry or cold!

Exploring caves is not only fun, but it can teach us about geology, biology and history. Some caves contain fossils, minerals and rare animals that can only be found in that one cave.

As you explore caves, you'll get to see some amazing things like underground lakes, sparkling mineral deposits and even some cave-dwelling animals like bats or spiders.

However, spelunking can be risky if not performed properly. It's important to be careful and respect the caves and their inhabitants by following the caving code:

Never go caving alone, bring the correct gear and equipment and never disturb plants or animals inside the cave.

Spelunking can be a thrilling and unforgettable experience, but it's not for everyone. You need to have a good level of fitness, know how to stay safe and take things slowly. If you'd like to go caving, find a trained caver or instructor who can teach you the ropes and help you to stay safe. Happy exploring!

Glossary

Adapted: Changed to fit a new environment.

Arthropods: Animals like insects, spiders and crabs with a hard outer body and jointed legs.

Deposits: Elements left in a place over time.

Eroded: Worn away over time.

Fossils: The remains of prehistoric plants or animals, found in rock.

Inhabitants: Beings that live in a specific place.

Navigate: To find a way from one place to another.

Prehistoric: The time before written records or history.

Rappelling: The act of moving down a steep, often rocky area using a rope.

Sonar: A way to find things by sending out sound waves and waiting for the sound to come back.

Spelunking: The activity of exploring caves.